SRA ART Connections

Professional Development Guide

SRA
Columbus, OH

The McGraw·Hill Companies

SRAonline.com

McGraw Hill SRA

Copyright © 2005 by SRA/McGraw-Hill.

All rights reserved. Permission is granted to reproduce the material contained herein on the condition that such material be reproduced only for classroom use; be provided to students, teachers, or families without charge; and be used solely in conjunction with *SRA Art Connections*. Any other reproduction, for use or sale, is prohibited without prior written permission from the publisher.

Send all inquiries to:
SRA/McGraw-Hill
8787 Orion Place
Columbus, OH 43240-4027

Printed in the United States of America.

ISBN 0-07-601857-1

2 3 4 5 6 7 8 9 MAZ 10 09 08 07 06 05

The McGraw-Hill Companies

Table of Contents

Introduction to Art 5
- Mini Course 6
- DBAE for the Elementary Classroom Teacher 7
- Introduction to Art History 10
- Getting Started 14
- Art and Cross Curricular Connections 15
- Classroom Management 17
- Art Assessment in the Elementary Classroom 19
- Safe Use of Art Materials 21

Art Education 25
- Mini Course 26
- Art Education in the United States 27
- Integrating Fine Arts 29
- Exhibiting Student Art 31
- Organizing the Art Room 33
- Museum Resources 34

Arts Advocacy 37
- Mini Course 38
- Arts Education Research Overview 39
- Arts Advocacy with Parents and the Community 40
- Grant Writing 41
- Web Resources 43

Introduction to Art

Mini Course

Take this short quiz to identify your strengths and weaknesses in art instruction. Choose the best answer for each question.

DBAE

1. Which of the following is not a discipline in Discipline-Based Art Education?

    a. Aesthetic perception   b. Art criticism
    c. Art elements   d. Art history

2. Which of the following is not part of art criticism?

    a. Interpreting the meaning of the artwork
    b. Comparing the artwork to other works
    c. Analyzing the elements and principles used in the work
    d. Describing the artwork

Art History

3. A common subject of prehistoric art is _____.

    a. farming   b. animals
    c. people   d. landscapes

4. The Renaissance began in _____.

    a. Germany   b. England
    c. France   d. Italy

5. Impressionist art is characterized by _____.

    a. small dabs of color
    b. precise, realistic images
    c. strong use of geometric shapes
    d. historical subject matter

6. Op art involves _____.

    a. minimal use of geometric shapes
    b. images of everyday objects, such as soup cans
    c. images that do not belong together
    d. precise use of art elements to create a visual illusion

Art Integration

7. Integrating visual arts with language arts can help students _____.

    a. make comparisons
    b. develop vocabulary
    c. use descriptive words
    d. all of the above

8. Concepts shared by art and mathematics include _____.

    a. prime numbers   b. patterning
    c. probability   d. none of the above

9. Art instruction helps students develop _____.

    a. creative thinking skills
    b. critical thinking skills
    c. problem solving skills
    d. all of the above

Safe Use of Art Materials

10. Products bearing the following symbol are safe for children to use.

    a. AP   b. UL
    c. MP   d. CD

11. Avoid using _____ with young children.

    a. water-based markers
    b. oil pastels
    c. permanent markers
    d. watercolors

12. Which adhesive should not be used with students?

    a. School glue   b. White paste
    c. Glue sticks   d. Rubber cement

Scoring: If you answered all the questions correctly, you have a good understanding of art education in the elementary classroom. You may want to read the next section on Art Education to expand your art education knowledge even further.

If you missed all the questions in one section, you might want to read the applicable article in order to achieve a better understanding.

If you missed more than eight questions, you could benefit from an introduction to art education. Consider reading all of the articles in the Introduction to Art section to get a basic understanding of art education in the elementary classroom.

Answers: 1. c, 2. b, 3. b, 4. d, 5. a, 6. d, 7. d, 8. b, 9. d, 10. a, 11. c, 12. d

Professional Development Guide

Discipline-Based Art Education for the Elementary Classroom Teacher

Rosalind Ragans, Ph.D.

There is much more to learning in art than making something nice to take home. Discipline-Based Art Education includes many different kinds of learning. Its foundation is based upon the four art disciplines: aesthetic perception; art criticism; art history; and art production.

Each of these art disciplines gives the student a different point of view from which to see, understand, and appreciate works of art as well as the cultures from which they come. Each of these disciplines is a recognized body of knowledge that is studied by professionals who perform in each area. Each of these disciplines is a domain of knowledge and skill that has been and continues to be developed by practitioners in each field: artists; art critics; art historians; and philosophers of art.

> Each of these art disciplines gives the student a different point of view from which to see, understand, and appreciate works of art as well as the cultures from which they come.

Discipline-Based Art Education is for all students, not just for the few who demonstrate talent in the production of art. It is designed to meet the needs of all who use it. It will help students understand art as a basic form of human culture and a basic means of human communication.

In the past, art was considered a nonacademic subject in which no serious learning took place. The art lesson was a time to relax and play with materials. It was a time for students to turn off their minds. Today, Discipline-Based Art Education supports the cognitive development of each student. It challenges the perceptual and intellectual development of each individual.

Aesthetic Perception

Aesthetics is a branch of philosophy. In visual art, aesthetics becomes the study of the nature of beauty and art. Aesthetics is concerned with the question: "What is art?" In the past, aesthetics was defined as the study of beauty because the creation of beauty was thought to be the purpose of art. Today, in our more complex society, the purpose of art has also become more complicated. Some aestheticians still believe that the purpose of art is to create beauty, or beautifully organized arrangements of the elements of art. Some believe that art must imitate reality. Others think of art as a strong means to communicate ideas and emotions. Students engage in aesthetic inquiry when they ask about the significance of a work of art, or when they question the value of a work.

Aesthetic concepts are the core of the **Art Connections** curriculum. They are the framework upon which all aspects of art learning are constructed. The About Aesthetic Perception section in the **Student** and **Teacher Editions** offers concrete methods for introducing students to aesthetics.

Art Criticism

Art criticism enables students to learn from works of art that have been created by artists from many cultures and time periods. Art criticism also provides a procedure that students can use to objectively study their own art products.

The four-step process of art criticism will help students expand their perceptive, analytical, interpretive, and aesthetic valuing abilities. The sequential steps of art criticism are similar to those used in the scientific method. During the first two steps, Describe and Analyze, students are asked to collect data objectively. During the third step, Interpret, students speculate about the meaning of the work based on the data collected; they make a hypothesis abut the idea, emotion, or mood expressed by the artist. During the fourth step, Decide or aesthetic judgment, the students offer their conclusions about the work of art.

Art criticism will help students study a work of art by noticing subject, composition, and meaning before making an aesthetic judgment. Too often, beginners look at a work of art briefly and immediately make a value judgment. The sequential procedures in art criticism force the students to postpone judgment while becoming immersed in the image. It forces them to have a fully funded visual experience.

> The sequential procedures in art criticism force the students to postpone judgment while becoming immersed in the image. It forces them to have a fully funded visual experience.

Detailed art criticism lessons are used to wrap up each unit in *Art Connections.* On these pages, the student is drawn into a deep study of a single work. During the analysis stage of this lesson, the concepts that were introduced in the unit are reviewed. Art criticism questions are also used as a self-assessment tool in each Creative Expression lesson.

Art History and Culture

During art criticism, the student learns from the work of art by studying the visual image itself. During the study of art history, the student learns about the work of art. Art history helps the student understand how the art functioned in its time and place. Students will study the history of art making in terms of styles and art movements. They will read the biographies of artists. They will consider the impact of time and place upon the artist and his or her work. As the students develop an understanding of art history, they comprehend the order of history through its visual images.

Art Connections is not an art history text, but any study of art should begin with learning something about the history of world art and the people who created it. Information about art history related to the featured works of art in each lesson is provided for the students throughout the text. Additional information is provided for the teacher in each lesson, and in ancillary materials such as the *Artist Profiles* books and on the backs of the *Large Prints.*

Art Production and Creative Expression

The making of art involves thoughts and skills. Students get ideas from observation, imagination, and emotions. They make images to express their ideas by the skillful manipulation of art media. During art production, students can become familiar with a wide range of art media, tools, equipment, and techniques. Students can learn about craftsmanship. They can express thoughts, values, and feelings in visual images. Students can learn about visual problem solving, and they can learn that there are an infinite number of right answers to the problem. Students learn to use divergent thinking as they work with art media.

Each *Art Connections* lesson includes an art production activity identified as Practice and Creative Expression in the *Student Edition.* This is the place for each student to creatively explore the lesson concept. Hands-on activities are often the most enjoyable aspect of art learning. The student

> DBAE challenges the students perceptually and intellectually. Students use their creativity while developing skills in perception, communication, imagination, judgment, and social understanding.

integrates and internalizes the verbal and visual concepts of the lesson during the creative manipulation of art materials. While every discipline in Discipline-Based Art Education is equally important, every discipline does not need equal time. Art production requires the longest amount of time.

Each production lesson has a self-assessment component using Art Criticism. The four steps of art criticism offer an objective procedure for thinking about the concepts and technical

Professional Development Guide

procedures used during the creation of art. Most students would be embarrassed to offer subjective statements about their own work or the work of classmates. But the objective questions offer them a chance to review their work without expressing personal feelings.

The Role of DBAE in the Elementary Classroom

Discipline-Based Art Education supports the goals of education in that it stimulates cognitive development. DBAE challenges the students perceptually and intellectually. Students use their creativity while developing skills in perception, communication, imagination, judgment, and social understanding. Art is an area of education in which problem solving and higher order thinking skills are developed. Art works well with all the various subjects studied in school.

Introduction to Art History

Throughout history, art has been a way for people to communicate their thoughts, feelings, and ideas. Is has reflected the social, political, and religious ideas of the time and place in which it was created. It not only expresses the personal ideas of the artist, but also conveys information about culture. Following is a brief summary of artistic media and styles through history.

Prehistoric Art
2 million B.C.–2000 B.C.

Prehistoric art was created before written history, and it often provides the only information we have about people who lived during this time.

One of the most familiar types of prehistoric art is cave paintings, which were created during the Paleolithic period (2 million B.C.–13,000 B.C.). Animals play an important role in most cave paintings, which often show scenes of people hunting stags, bison, and mammoths. Horses frequently appear in cave paintings. Scholars have different theories about the purpose of these paintings; some believe the paintings were made to prepare for a hunt, while others suggest that they celebrated a successful hunt.

Prehistoric people gradually moved out of caves and began to construct their own dwellings. Small communities formed, and people began to farm and domesticate animals. During the Neolithic period (7000 B.C.–2000 B.C.), people also constructed large stone monuments. The most famous of these monuments is Stonehenge in England; however, similar monuments were constructed in other parts of Europe, Asia, and North America. Scientists are not sure how primitive people were able to cut, transport, and raise these stones, which can weigh more than 50 tons.

Famous works: Cave paintings at Lascaux, France; Stonehenge

Ancient Civilizations
3000 B.C.–A.D. 500

In Mesopotamia (present-day Syria and Iraq), the Sumerians developed a system of writing called *Cuneiform.* Their art included small, realistic sculptures. Their architecture included ziggurats, or temples made of brick-covered mountains with exterior staircases. Another Mesopotamian civilization, the Assyrians, created precise relief carvings in stone. The reliefs were richly painted and often depicted scenes of royal life, hunts, and animals.

The Egyptian civilization developed along the banks of the Nile River. Religion played a major role in Egyptian life and art; artists created elaborate decorations inside tombs and temples.

In the Indus river valley, the Indian civilization arose. The Indians built large cities that were home to thousands of people. Their earliest artists carved small relief sculptures in soapstone. Again, animals were a popular subject matter. Indian architects built stupas, which were dome-shaped places of worship.

The Chinese civilization developed along the Yellow River. The ancient Chinese invented paper and porcelain, and developed the process of woodblock painting. They also created detailed works in cast bronze. Later Chinese artists excelled at calligraphy (beautiful writing), and eventually began using their calligraphy brushes to paint pictures.

Greece is considered the birthplace of western civilization. Greek artists and architects tried to achieve ideal proportions in their works; their buildings were based on mathematical proportions, and their sculptures represented their idea of the perfect human form. The Romans adapted Greek art to their own needs, creating arched buildings and beautiful interior decorations.

Famous works: Pyramids at Giza, Parthenon

> Throughout history, art has been a way for people to communicate their thoughts, feelings, and ideas.

Art of Asia, Africa, and the Americas
A.D. 500–A.D. 1500

Chinese artists were among the first to recognize painting pictures as a worthy pursuit, and created beautiful landscapes. They also produced religious sculptures and highly-prized works in porcelain. In Japan, architects built intricate and richly-decorated temples out of wood. The Japanese also created large-scale sculptures, often of the Buddha. Although early Japanese paintings showed influences from other Asian cultures, Japanese artists eventually developed a uniquely Japanese style of painting, and also excelled at woodblock printing.

Islamic art arose after the birth of Muhammad in Mecca in A.D. 570, and often contains intricate lines, shapes, and patterns. Islamic artists created elaborate decorations in mosques and in books.

African art includes a rich tradition in sculpture. The Yoruba people of Nigeria created lifelike sculpture portraits of their rulers. Artists in Benin (present-day Nigeria) created relief sculptures from cast metal that decorated the walls of the royal palace.

The Mayan civilization arose in the Yucatán peninsula (present-day Belize, Guatemala, and Honduras). Although Mayan artists created clay figures and relief carvings, they are best known for their huge temples. The Aztecs also built temples, some of which were carved into the sides of mountains. The artists of the Inca civilization (present-day Peru) were expert builders, and they were able to create structures in which a knife blade could not fit between the stones.

Famous works: Great Buddha at Kamakura; Taj Mahal

The Middle Ages
A.D. 500–A.D. 1500

At the end of the Roman Empire, Asian, African, and American art began to develop, and Europe experienced a period called the Middle Ages. After the fall of Rome, religion became the driving force in European life. During the early part of the Middle Ages, buildings still included Roman features such as rounded arches and heavy walls. By the twelfth century, however, a shift occurred. People began to move from rural areas to cities, wealthy merchant classes developed, and artists formed craft guilds. The Gothic style arose, which featured tall buildings with pointed arches, elaborate stained-glass windows, and richly decorated interiors.

Famous works: Bayeux Tapestry, Westminster Abbey, Notre Dame (Paris)

The Renaissance
A.D. 1500–A.D. 1600

Toward the end of the Middle Ages, the invention of the printing press and the exploration of the Americas helped reawaken interest in exploring not only new places, but also new ideas. A growing merchant class provided a new market for artwork. Artists still created religious works as they had during the Middle Ages, but they also began to work with secular themes from the world around them. This new movement was called the Renaissance.

The Renaissance began in Italy and gradually spread to other parts of Europe. Artists studied the artwork of Greece and Rome and tried to create lifelike works. Many artists, including Michelangelo and Leonardo da Vinci, studied science and mathematics in addition to art. The first prominent women artists emerged during this time.

Famous artists: Botticelli, Albrecht Dürer, Michelangelo, Raphael, Leonardo da Vinci

The Seventeenth, Eighteenth, and Nineteenth Centuries
A.D. 1600–A.D. 1900

The three hundred years after the Renaissance saw several movements and styles emerge in the Western art world. The first of these was the **baroque** style, which emphasized movement and emotion. Like baroque music, baroque art was dramatic, rich, and complex. Subject matter ranged from religious scenes to images of everyday life.

As the eighteenth century began, **rococo** emerged as the dominant artistic style. Unlike the complex and sometimes dark baroque art, rococo art was more lighthearted and emphasized graceful movement and delicate colors. Subject matter ranged from idealized scenes to landscapes and even portraits.

After the American and French revolutions, **neoclassicism** grew in popularity. Neoclassicism

Professional Development Guide

once again imitated the formal design ideas of the Greeks and Romans, and emphasized realistic images and heroic events. A great deal of early American architecture was built in the neoclassical style, including Monticello (Thomas Jefferson's home) and the White House.

At the beginning of the nineteenth century, artists began painting in a different style as people looked to art for distraction from the political situation of the times. **Romanticism** emphasized rich color and strong emotion. The music and literature of this time also focused on feelings instead of historical ideals.

One group of artists thought that art should portray issues in a realistic manner, but without glorifying the past. This movement became known as **realism,** and presented contemporary scenes in a realistic manner. The growth of photography also fueled this interest in showing places and events as they actually appeared.

Impressionism is one of the most well known artistic movements of this period. Like the realists, impressionists painted the world around them. Unlike realists, however, impressionists focused on how light affected an image instead of the shape of the image. Instead of painting the image as it might appear in a photograph, they used small strokes of color to capture how the image looked at a given moment in time.

The term **post-impressionism** is used to describe a variety of individual painting styles that arose after the impressionist movement. Some artists, including Paul Cézanne, used blocks of color instead of small strokes; this allowed them to portray shapes that were more realistic while still exploring the play of light and color. Other artists, such as Vincent van Gogh, cared less about visual accuracy than about conveying a mood or feeling.

While European artists practiced these various styles, art in other parts of the world evolved as well. In Africa, artists of the Asante kingdom (Ghana) were master goldsmiths who created elaborate jewelry. Also in Africa, weavers began to create Kente cloth with rich colors and complex patterns. In North America, various Native American nations created works of art unique to their geographical area. The Inuit of Alaska and Canada created detailed carvings in walrus ivory. The people of the Pacific Northwest carved huge totem poles. The Pueblo people of the Southwest excelled at pottery using local clay, and Navajo artists created loom weavings with intricate patterns and bold colors.

Famous artists: Frans Hals, Rembrandt, Jan Vermeer (baroque); Thomas Gainsborough, Francisco Goya, Jean-Antoine Watteau (rococo); Jaques-Louis David (neoclassicism); William Blake, Joseph M.W. Turner (romanticism); Édouard Manet (realism); Claude Monet (impressionism); Paul Cézanne, Vincent van Gogh (post-impressionism); Maria Martinez (Pueblo pottery)

Art of the Twentieth Century
A.D. 1900–present

With the growth of photography in the second half of the nineteenth century, artists no longer bore the primary responsibility of recording the time and place in which they lived. This brought about a shift in the way many people looked at art, and encouraged artists to experiment with new and different styles. Some artists explored several styles during their lifetime.

Expressionism began in Germany and emphasized feelings and emotion. These artists were more interested in expressing true feelings than in classic notions of beauty. Many of these artists experienced the difficult times surrounding World War I and did not shy away from portraying emotions such as fear and anger.

Cubism was based in France and emphasized structure in artwork. Cubists tried to simplify and manipulate shape and form in their artwork.

Surrealism used fantasy to convey emotion. Although surrealist works appear very detailed and lifelike, the paintings contain images that don't belong together or that would not occur in the real world.

As European artists experimented with these styles, a group of American artists decided to focus on American themes. These **regionalist** artists painted scenes of American working people, whether in cities or in rural areas.

After World War II, New York City became the capital of the art world. The first new style to emerge there was **abstract expressionism,** which focused on the elements and principles in a work of art instead of a recognizable subject.

Artists of the **pop art** movement used images of popular culture, such as soup cans and comic strips, in a variety of artwork. They encouraged people to look at everyday objects with the object's appearance in mind instead of its function. **Op art** artists used precise arrangements of the elements of art such as line and color to create the illusion of movement.

Minimalist artists tried to keep their works very simple, concentrating on color or shape as the main element in the work. Minimalist sculptors used only a few geometric forms in their works. Minimalist art is not meant to represent any emotion or object; the focus is the artwork itself.

Famous artists: Wassily Kandinsky, Käthe Kollwitz (expressionism); Pablo Picasso (cubism); Salvador Dali, René Magritte (surrealism); Thomas Hart Benton, Grant Wood (regionalism); Helen Frankenthaler, Jackson Pollock, Mark Rothko (abstract expressionism); Roy Lichtenstein, Andy Warhol (pop art); Bridget Riley (op art); Frank Stella (minimalism)

Getting Started

Knowing your fine art materials and planning how you will use them can help you incorporate art instruction into your classroom seamlessly throughout the school year. Below are some suggestions for taking stock of your art materials and preparing for art instruction.

Before School Begins

1. Explore the components you have (***Student Editions, Overhead Transparencies, Large Prints,*** and so on). Consider primary and alternative uses for each of the components. For example, you could use the ***Overhead Transparencies*** to teach concepts during each lesson or to reinforce those concepts at the end of a unit. You could display the ***Large Prints*** in your room throughout the school year, or you could display only the prints that correspond to the unit you are teaching.

2. Plan your year.

   - Consider how often you will teach art to the students, and how long each art instruction session will be.
   - Decide how many lessons you can present. Be sure to include preparation and clean-up time in your calculations. The ***Art Connections Teacher Editions*** provide estimated times for each lesson in the program.
   - Examine your curriculum requirements. Most states have standards for fine art instruction at the state and/or district level.
   - Select the lessons that best meet your curriculum requirements.

3. Organize your art materials.

   - First identify the Creative Expression activities that you will have students do and compile a list of materials. The ***Art Connections Teacher Editions*** provide a lesson materials list at the beginning of each lesson; unit materials are included in each Unit Planning Guide.
   - Determine how you will budget materials to last the entire year, and order your materials. See the article "The Community as a Resource for Art Materials" on page T13 of the ***Art Connections Teacher Edition*** for suggestions on how to obtain art materials at little or no cost.

4. Arrange classroom space to create and store student artwork. Students can work on Creative Expression activities at their desks or at art tables, depending on the materials used in the activity. Student artwork should be stored flat in student portfolios. Encourage students to personalize the fronts of their portfolios with their names, drawings, and so on.

The First Day of School

1. Introduce students to the art program. Display several ***Large Prints*** in the room. Explain to students that they will learn about works of art and the artists who made them, and that they will make their own artwork throughout the year.

2. Introduce the art area to students. Show them where they can find supplies. Hand out empty portfolios and let students decorate them.

3. Discuss with students rules for behavior, handling art materials, and cleaning up.

4. Begin the ***Art Connections*** introductory lessons, including What Is Art?, About Art Criticism, About Aesthetic Perception, About Art History and Culture, and About Creative Expression.

Planning a Lesson

1. Review the lesson in the ***Teacher Edition,*** including the lesson objectives, in-text questions, the Practice activity, and the Creative Expression activity. Practice the activities if you have not done them before. (Tips and visual aides for each activity are provided in the Activity Tips section of the ***Student Edition*** and ***Teacher Edition.***)

2. Assemble program components, such as ***Overhead Transparencies, Large Prints,*** or ***Big Books.***

3. Make copies of any assessments or blackline masters that will be needed for the lesson.

4. Assemble the art materials.

5. Determine how you will assess the lesson. ***Art Connections*** provides several assessment options for each lesson.

Art and Cross Curricular Connections

Tina Farrell

The study and production of artwork enhances learning in all areas of the curriculum. When teachers and students connect art to their other subjects, learning occurs in the natural and interrelated way that it exists in the real world. We know from experience that learning is most meaningful when it is interconnected—not isolated. Therefore, making the natural connections that exist within each discipline of study and art enhances total understanding and brings meaning to fragmented information.

Below are just a few of the ways that art education can impact the study of other subjects.

Reading/Language Arts

In the viewing and analysis of a work of art, students develop oral and written communication skills. Teachers can enhance the language process by writing art terms and concepts on the board, having students generate lists of adjectives and adverbs to describe artworks, encouraging reflective inquiry into art, having students read about art and artists, and having students use works of art as stimuli for all forms of writing. This helps students:

- develop vocabulary
- record ideas and feelings
- distinguish between fact and opinion
- use descriptive words
- make comparisons
- develop their skills in usage and grammar
- acquire skills in writing for a variety of purposes

Mathematics

Mathematics concepts are enhanced through art. When math concepts are presented or expressed in a visual or manipulative manner, students can more easily grasp them. The comparison and development of shapes and forms, visual-spatial relationships, measurement, proportion, estimation, and grids and graphs, for example, all are best explained through art. Art education helps reinforce such essential math skills as:

- patterning
- attributes of geometric shapes and solids
- number
- measurement
- problem solving
- reasoning

Science

In the art-making process, children learn that multiple ways to solve problems exist. They learn to discover, imagine, try new materials and techniques, experiment, develop and test hypotheses, and observe and record visual data. These are many of the skills, objectives, and habits of mind taught in science. Through artwork, students can also visualize science concepts such as:

- characteristics of organisms
- structures of life
- behavior
- change
- observation
- interpreting and analyzing data

Social Studies

The history of the world is reflected in the functional and aesthetic works of art produced by the peoples of the world. Children can gain great insights about near and distant cultures through the study of art, artifacts, and architecture. Learning about artwork and artists also involves students in:

- history
- geography
- social relationships
- cultural contributions
- analyzing and interpreting information

The Arts

The arts all complement each other in the skills, elements, principles, and beliefs that are emphasized in each discipline. Each area presents a unique way to express ideas and transform emotions into song, dance, interactions, words, and images. Visual artists research, develop rough drafts (sketches), plan, develop ideas, produce completed visual ideas, and sign and title their works. These are the processes that authors, writers, dancers, composers, actors, and poets also employ.

Life Skills

In art, children develop craftsmanship, self-discipline, dedication to a task, skills for working both individually and cooperatively, and pride in one's work. These skills are necessary for success in any area of their lives.

Critical Thinking Skills

Studying the visual arts develops higher-level thinking skills as students analyze, compare, interpret, synthesize, and make inferences and judgments about works of art.

Art is a great integrating subject because art, first and foremost, is a form of human communication. Art is one of the first forms of communication for children. Children often express complex ideas through visual symbols that represent their beginning language system. Art is a vehicle for children to learn about the world around them and to organize the information in a comprehensive format. As young children draw, they take textures, shapes, and colors from a complex world and form them into coherent visual images. This visual cognition, a powerful way for children to process information, is the basis for learning in and through art.

Classroom Management

Bunyan Morris
Art Teacher, Effingham County School System, Georgia

While motivating students to express themselves visually through creative means, the elementary teacher is challenged with the task of maintaining proper classroom management. The purpose of this article is to provide some practical methods of motivating creative thought and action under the guidance of successful classroom management. Combine these methods with your own to give students the best learning experience possible.

Be Prepared

Begin the art lesson excited and ready. If you set the tone at the beginning and grasp immediate control, it will be much easier to keep it throughout the lesson. It is important to have art prints and demonstration materials ready and in place for the initial focus. Practice an activity before demonstrating it if you have not yet taught the activity. Even if you have taught art in your classroom, it might be a good idea to practice if there is a concept or an activity that has not been taught in a long time.

Focus

For the initial focus of the lesson, gather the students into a group on the floor or in an area of the classroom that is ready for discussion and demonstration. By gathering the students into a compact group, it is easier to make eye contact and to keep the attention of all learners. If there is no room for a separate demonstration and discussion spot, gather the desks into a closer group so that no one is "out of reach."

Introduce the Art

Always introduce a lesson with a work of art that relates to what the students will be learning. Students get excited playing detective. Finding clues and ideas in a painting or sculpture allows them to make their own interpretations and assessments about art. They will in turn learn to apply this to their own work. Encouraging them to ask questions and share ideas about a work will give the students motivation and fresh ideas to take into the Creative Expression portion of the lesson.

Moving to Creative Expression

Always control the manner in which the students move to the project area from the demonstration/discussion center. Release the students in a manner that will keep order but not quell their enthusiasm about the lesson. Use positive reinforcement by complimenting those who are sitting quietly, and send them first. It will not take long for the others to catch on. After time, most of the students will become conditioned to this expectation. Even if they've been involved in a lively discussion, they will automatically become settled as this transitional period approaches.

Classroom Design

Not only should the students be orderly, but the classroom must also be organized and conducive to the movement of the teacher and students. The Creative Expression areas should have enough space between them for the teacher to reach every student. There should be enough space in traffic areas for student movement. The supplies should be organized on leveled shelves so that students will return them to their proper places. If the teacher keeps the room and supplies organized, hopefully the students will too.

As well as keeping the room and supplies organized, the rest of the room should be visually pleasing. Display student art and master prints in your classroom. This builds self-esteem. When possible, display every child's work. Keep interesting objects about the room for visual reference. These objects might include plants, old toys, or anything that might capture the attention and interest of your students. Use these objects in still lifes and as objects of visual reference for lines, shapes, and other elements and principles of art.

When moving about the room assisting students, it is important to keep the senses alive and to be aware of what is happening with the other students. See and hear what they think you can't.

Closing the Lesson

Normally one should try to close the lesson with a review of the lesson's objectives. This should be short and interesting. This is also the time to reward the students for good behavior. The teacher must set the criteria for earning the award. Do not give the award if it is not earned. Of course, the students must be aware of the opportunity to earn an award ahead of time. One method that works is to award the students with a "Super Behavior Card." After earning a certain number of Super Behavior Cards, students can be rewarded with a party or extra time at recess.

Hopefully these ideas and suggestions will reduce the challenge of maintaining classroom control and motivating students. The teacher must decide what works best for each situation. All of the motivation and management techniques here have been tried and have been proved to work. They may not work for everyone, but combined with one's individual strategies, they will increase the probability of success in the classroom.

A Sampling of Art Games for Home or School

Art Lotto: National Gallery of Art. Safari Limited, Miami, Florida.

ARTDECK. Aristoplay, Ann Arbor, Michigan.

The Fine Art Game. Piatnik, Wiener Spielkartenfabrik, Ferd. PIATNIK & Söhne.

Where Art Thou? WJ Fantasy, Inc., Bridgeport, Connecticut.

Art Assessment in the Elementary Classroom

Assessment in art can be problematic for a variety of reasons. Many teachers are reluctant to evaluate a student's creative expression in a work of art as good or bad. Because there are often no right or wrong answers, students and their parents could challenge a teacher's subjective opinion of a work if it were reflected in a letter grade. Furthermore, many classroom teachers do not feel qualified to grade student artwork. In addition, teachers do not want to discourage creative expression by giving a low grade or an undeserved grade. People also often feel that talented students have the advantage in art and that students should not be evaluated on how talented they are, but rather on how much effort they put into their work and how much progress they make.

All of these assessment troubles stem from a focus on art production rather than a reflection of art history and culture, aesthetics, or art criticism. A broader focus in teaching art and a variety of assessment options may help teachers as they assess students' learning in art.

Assessment of Lesson Objectives

Instead of subjective opinions of whether or not one likes a student's artwork, students can be evaluated on whether or not they met the art lesson objectives or demonstrated the knowledge and skills introduced in the lesson. In a quality art program, there are objectives for aesthetic perception, art history, and art criticism, as well as for demonstrating understanding of the elements and principles of art in art production.

In *Art Connections,* every lesson has four clear, measurable objectives. At the end of each lesson, a rubric provides evaluation criteria for each objective.

Art Production: Evaluating Student Artwork

Teachers frequently evaluate student artwork on the basis of how well it reflects the elements and principles of art that are being stressed in the lesson and how well the student met the criteria for the artwork. Some teachers make up rubrics or standards for the artwork beforehand and tell students how their work will be evaluated at the time it is assigned. Other teachers use written or mental checklists of their standards as they look at student artwork. Teachers may use this evaluation as an opportunity to discuss the work with the student and find out whether the student thought he or she met the objectives for the artwork.

In *Art Connections,* teachers can also use the Assessment Masters in the *Assessment* book to get an idea of whether a student understands the elements or principles of art for the lesson.

Art Criticism and Aesthetic Perception: Self- and Peer-Assessment

The four-step process of art criticism (Describe, Analyze, Interpret, Decide) provides a procedure that students can use to objectively study their own art products as well as the works of others. The sequential steps of art criticism are similar to those used in the scientific method. During the first two steps, Describe and Analyze, students collect data objectively. During the third step, Interpret, students think about the meaning of the work based on the data collected; they make a hypothesis about the idea, emotion, or mood expressed by the artist. During the fourth step, Decide, the students offer their aesthetic judgment about the work of art. The sequential procedures in art criticism force the students to postpone judgment while becoming immersed in the image. It forces them to have a fully funded visual experience before drawing conclusions about a work.

Art Connections includes art criticism questions for every Creative Expression activity. Additionally, the Aesthetic Perception feature in every lesson of the *Student Edition* provides students with an opportunity to evaluate their developing aesthetic perception.

Professional Development Guide

Art History and Culture

Art is a visual record of history and diverse cultures. The goals for elementary art education are that students understand and appreciate different historical periods, cultures, and artistic styles and develop respect for the traditions and contributions of diverse societies.

In *Art Connections,* every lesson introduces a piece of fine art from a particular culture, time, and style. In the Introducing the Art strategies, teachers are encouraged to compare, contrast, and share the Art History and Culture information as well as the information provided in the *Artist Profiles* book to help students develop an understanding of the visual arts in relation to history and cultures. Through discussion and elements in student artwork, teachers can evaluate students' awareness in this area.

Portfolio Assessment

Teachers who include art in their curriculum could claim to have inspired the growing use of portfolio assessment in other subject areas. Many teachers collect the best examples of a student's work and look at the progress over time. They display it and discuss it with students and parents. Student art journals that are filled with ideas, drawings, and sketches also provide an opportunity for portfolio assessment.

In *Art Connections,* students are encouraged to keep their best work in a Student Portfolio and to maintain an Art Journal. Reminders of these types of portfolio assessments appear in the *Teacher Edition.*

Performance Assessment

Unlike other subject areas, art education has a long tradition of performance assessment. In art class, students make things to demonstrate what they can do. In quality art programs, teachers use performance descriptions for not only art production, but also art criticism, art history and culture, and aesthetic perception to aid them in evaluating student demonstrations of knowledge and skills in art.

In *Art Connections,* every work of art a student produces can be considered for performance assessment of the lesson concept. Performance assessments can also involve discussions about the works of art to introduce the lesson concept and art criticism questions.

Art not only enables teachers to evaluate student knowledge and skills in art each year, but it also provides a wonderful opportunity to assess a student's growth and development over time. Students and parents are often reluctant to discard artwork and fondly review it from time to time to see how children's ideas and skills have changed. Schools often keep an example of student artwork in a student's portfolio from year to year.

A thoughtful and fair art assessment program enables teachers to really see how much their students are capable of accomplishing.

References

Armstrong, Carmen L. *Designing Assessment in Art.* Reston, VA: The National Art Education Association. 1994.

Into the Portfolio Process: A Handbook for student Assessment. California Art Education Association, Butte County Office of Education. 1995.

Rudner, Lawrence M. and Carol Boston. *A Look at Performance Assessment for Art Education.* Reston, VA: The National Art Education Association. 1994.

Safe Use of Art Materials

Mary Ann Boykin
Director, The Art School for Children and Young Adults, University of Houston–Clear Lake, Texas

Elementary teachers are responsible for the safety of their students. To ensure safety in art class, teachers need to be aware of safety issues that can affect the well-being of the children they teach, as well as themselves. Specific safety standards have been established by the Center for Safety in the Arts, and these guidelines should be carefully followed to assure that neither the children nor their teachers are injured by the use of unsafe art materials.

Elementary teachers should do two things to prevent problems. The first is to keep all toxic and hazardous substances out of the classroom. The second is to know how to use the materials safely, because any materials can become hazardous when used inappropriately.

Toxic Substances

A toxic substance is defined by the Center for Occupational Hazards as "a poison which can damage your body's organ systems when you are overexposed to it." This harm can be immediate or can be the result of repeated exposure over time. Toxic substances can enter the body in three ways: absorption through the skin; inhalation through the nose or mouth; or ingestion through eating or drinking in the area where toxic materials are being used. It is up to the teacher to make sure toxic substances do not enter the classroom and that all materials are used safely to avoid problems.

Pregnant women and those who are nursing infants must be especially careful to prevent exposure to toxic substances. Fumes, sprays, dusts, and powders present a real hazard to the fetus, can be transferred to the infant through the mother's milk, and can be carried home to the infant or young child through dusts and residue picked up by clothing and hair. The safe path is to completely avoid exposure to any toxin by carefully reading labels and applying common sense to the situation. For example, if you plan to work with chalks or clay, the safe method would include use of a respirator mask, which would prevent inhalation of these substances.

Children and Safe Art Materials

Preschool and elementary children are particularly vulnerable to unsafe art materials for a variety of reasons. Their lower body weight allows a toxic substance to be more concentrated in their bodies. In addition, because children have a more rapid metabolism than adults, toxic substances are more quickly absorbed into their bodies.

Children also tend to have more hand-to-mouth contact than adults, which allows accidental as well as purposeful ingestion of toxic materials. Furthermore, children are easily distracted from safety warnings regarding materials as they become involved in the art process. The tendency of children to have cuts and scratches also allows for ready entry of toxins into their bodies.

What the Labels Mean

Since 1990 our government has required the labeling of all hazardous materials. Any product labeled as hazardous is totally inappropriate for the elementary school. Safe art materials carry the statement that the material "Conforms to ASTMD-4236." A simple "nontoxic" statement on a product is not adequate.

The Arts and Crafts Materials Institute developed a voluntary program to provide a safe standard for materials used by children. Products bearing the labels AP (Approved Product) or CP (Certified Product) have actually been tested by toxicologists in major universities and have been deemed safe for children to use. The HL (Health Label) on art products indicates that these products are appropriate to use with children 12-years-old or older under the supervision of a teacher. Products with HL labels are not safe for elementary children.

Safe Art Materials

The following are guidelines for choosing and using basic art materials in a safe manner.

Drawing Materials

Markers

- Use only water-soluble AP- or CP-designated markers. Permanent markers are extremely dangerous and can cause lung and liver damage if inhaled. Never use permanent markers in the elementary classroom.
- The use of scented markers is also discouraged. This teaches children to sniff or smell materials.

Chalks

Use only dustless chalk. Most chalks are better used outside for sidewalk art. The amount of dust created in a classroom by twenty children wiping and blowing chalk can be irritating to those who suffer from allergies, asthma, and other respiratory problems.

Crayons

Use oil pastels; the colors are richer and the satisfaction is greater! Crayons should also bear the AP or CP label to ensure that no lead is present in these materials.

Painting Materials

- Use only liquid tempera and/or watercolor paints. If you must use powdered tempera paints, mix these outside and have the paints ready before children enter the classroom. Avoid inhaling the powders of tempera colors.
- Do not use any spray paints or fixatives. These are extremely dangerous.

Printmaking Materials

- Use only water-soluble printer's inks. Do not use any solvent-based inks.
- Use pencils to carve into unused foam trays for a printing block. Do not use mat knives or other sharp instruments.

Collage Materials

Scissors

Sharp scissors should not be used by young children; blunt points are safe. Fourth and fifth graders may use rounded points with teacher supervision.

Glue and Paste

Use only school paste or white glue for adhering papers. Do not use rubber cement unless it bears the AP or CP label. Do not use any solvent-based glues.

Sculpture and Three-Dimensional Materials

Clay

- Use premixed, moist clay for sculpture and pottery. Do not allow students to take home any unfired clay.
- Remind students to wash their hands thoroughly after using clay. The residual dust can be harmful and irritating if inhaled.
- Paint clay pieces with tempera or watercolor paints.

Glazes

Do not use glazes. Some have the approved labels, but they are not recommended for elementary use.

Carving Tools

Use pencils, craft sticks, or other blunt tools to carve clay. Soapstone should not be used for carving in a closed environment.

Papier-Mâché

Read labels carefully on pastes used for papier-mâché because some pastes contain pesticides or preservatives that are extremely harmful.

Stitchery, Weaving, and Fiber Materials

- Use blunt plastic needles and loosely woven fabrics such as burlap for stitchery. Blunt metal tapestry needles are safe if supervised.
- Young children will have trouble cutting fabric and yarns with their scissors. Precut some lengths of yarn prior to introducing the task.

General Safety Precautions for Art

- Read the labels on all materials used in the art room. Look carefully for the AP/CP labels. If these are not present, be suspicious. Imported art materials should be looked upon with extreme caution. Other countries have not developed the rigid safety codes adopted by the United States.

- Do not accept or use old art materials that may have been left in the school or donated by some well-meaning adult. If the materials do not bear the current safety codes, toss them out!

- Never allow food or drink in the room where art activities are being conducted. Dust and even fibers float freely in the air and can readily contaminate food.

- Practice cleanliness. Have children wash their hands thoroughly with soap after using art materials.

- Use absolutely no permanent markers or solvent-based materials in the art room. If a material stains the clothes or hands and does not clean up with simple soap and water, it is not appropriate or safe for young children to use.

- Use plastic containers for washing brushes; glass is dangerous in the hands of young children.

- Paper cutters should not be used by elementary children. The paper cutter should be kept in a locked position always with the blade turned to the wall or out of students' reach.

- Do not use commercial dyes with children; use vegetable or natural dyes (flowers, teas, onion skins).

- Do not allow children in the room where a kiln is firing; both the heat and the fumes are dangerous.

References

Babin, A., Editor, *Art Hazards News*, Vol. 17, No. 5, 1994.

Babin, A., Peltz, P.A., Rossol, M. "Children's Art Supplies Can Be Toxic." New York: Center for Safety in the Arts, 1992.

McCann, Michael. *Artist Beware*. New York: Watson-Guptil Publications, 1979.

McCann, Michael. "Hazards in the Arts." New York: Center for safety in the Arts, 1989.

Qualley, Charles A. *Safety in the Art Room*. Massachusetts: Davis Publications, Inc., 1986.

For further information:

Center for Safety in the Arts
5 Beekman Street, Suite 820
New York, New York 10038

(212) 227-6220

Art Education

Mini Course

Take this short quiz to identify your strengths and weaknesses in art instruction. Choose the best answer for each question.

Art Education in the United States

1. A primary champion of Discipline-Based Art Education was ___.

   a. The Getty Museum
   b. The Metropolitan Museum of Art
   c. The National Gallery of Art
   d. The Museum of Fine Arts, Boston

2. National standards for art education were first published in ___.

   a. 1944 b. 1964
   c. 1994 d. 2004

Integrating Fine Arts

3. Line is an element in ___.

   a. visual arts b. dance
   c. music d. all of the above

4. A tableau in theatre is similar to a ___ in visual art.

   a. still life b. sculpture
   c. collage d. landscape

Exhibiting Student Art/Organizing the Art Room

5. Before displaying student artwork, you should ___.

   a. ask the student's permission
   b. correct any errors
   c. write the student's name on the work
   d. frame the work

6. Student artwork may be displayed ___.

   a. in the classroom
   b. in a school gallery
   c. in the administrative offices
   d. all of the above

7. Including a listening center in the art room ___.

   a. helps students focus on teacher demonstrations
   b. protects books from damage
   c. keeps students from being distracted by art materials
   d. all of the above

8. Which item is not essential in an elementary art room?

   a. kiln b. production area
   c. storage d. display area

Museum Resources

9. Museums can provide which of the following services?

   a. Guided tours
   b. Educational materials
   c. Online resources
   d. All of the above

10. Before going on a museum visit, you should ___.

    a. obtain teacher packets from the museum
    b. plan to lead the tour yourself
    c. visit the exhibit yourself
    d. develop an assignment that allows your students to reflect on the experience

. . . .

Answers: 1. a, 2. c, 3. d, 4. b, 5. a, 6. d, 7. d, 8. a, 9. d, 10. c

Scoring:
If you answered all the questions correctly, you have a good understanding of elementary art education. You may want to read the next section on Arts Advocacy to expand your art education knowledge even further.

If you missed all the questions in one section, you might want to read the applicable article in order to achieve a better understanding.

If you missed more than seven questions, you could benefit from more information on art education. Consider reading all of the articles in the Art Education section to get a better understanding of elementary art education.

Art Education in the United States

Rosalind Ragans, Ph.D.

The public schools in America reflect the culture and values of our people. Early Americans did not grow up in a world of artistic and architectural traditions. Aesthetic and artistic concerns were not important because survival and practical tasks took time and energy. In Europe, the aristocracy were the patrons of the arts. Our democracy produced businessmen and politicians who were concerned with the practical. To them the arts were a "frill" to be considered only after the real work was done. It is only in the last decades that art education has progressed to a point where it is being considered an essential part of education.

The origins of art education in the United States are related to the needs of the business world in mid-nineteenth century New England. Business leaders saw how the English had revitalized their schools of design in order to compete with European business in taste, style, and aesthetic quality. American business leaders brought Walter Smith to the U.S. and appointed him director of drawing in the public schools of Boston. Smith developed a sequential curriculum for industrial drawing. He published books for instructional purposes. In them the lessons led teachers and students through a rigid sequence of drawing lessons that involved rote learning, copying, and repetition. Although we would reject his program today, he gave art education a firm footing in the schools.

At the beginning of the twentieth century, Cizek focused on creative art activities for young children. During the 1920s, the teachings of John Dewey also placed an emphasis on creativity and play as developmental tools.

Wesley Dow sought to develop a systematic way to teach the structure of art at Columbia University. In Chicago, Walter Sargent focused on the process by which children learned to draw. In the 1920s, the picture-study movement began the study of art appreciation.

In the 1930s, the Otawanna Art Project in Minnesota was a community-based project that promoted the application of the principles of art in everyday life. In Europe, the Bauhaus was a professional art school committed to integrating technology into the artists' work. Many teachers who were fleeing the Nazis in Europe brought the Bauhaus philosophy of design to America.

In the 1950s, Victor Loenfeld's *Creative and Mental Growth* was published. This promoted the creative development of children. This was the strongest influence in shaping art education through the 1960s, but in the everyday classrooms, art still remained a "make-and-do" holiday craft activity.

In the 1960s, one of the most influential leaders in educational thinking was Jerome Bruner who proposed a spiraling, sequencing of concepts in every field of learning. This approach to teaching was introduced into art education by Manuel Barkan. He called for students to be exposed to a wide range of learning activities in art. The Kettering Project at Stanford University, led by Elliot Eisner, featured foundational art "domains" (production, criticism, and history) as the source of content. Other projects such as CEMRL and SWRL developed materials for teaching about critical and historical concepts in art.

During the 1970s and 1980s, art educators across the country were looking for a way to structure their curricula. States began to revise outdated curriculum guides. The term "Discipline-Based Art Education" first appeared in 1984 in an article by Dwaine Greer. Promoted by the Getty, DBAE became a major force in art education and influenced national standards for the arts published in 1994.

Discipline-Based Art Education is a format for organizing learning in art education. It is based upon four basic art disciplines: aesthetic perception, art history and culture, creative expression, and art criticism.

In visual art, aesthetics is the study of the nature of beauty and art. Some aestheticians believe that the purpose of art is to create beauty, or to beautifully

Professional Development Guide

arrange the elements and principles of art. Others think of art as a means to communicate ideas and emotions. Students engage in **aesthetic perception** and inquiry when they ask about the significance of a work of art, or when they question the value of a work.

During the study of **art history,** students learn about a work of art and about how the art functioned in its time and place. Students learn about the artist and consider the impact of time and place upon his or her work. As students develop an understanding of art history, they understand more about general history through its visual images.

Creative expression involves not only creative skills, but also critical thinking skills. Students make images to express their ideas by the skillful manipulation of art media. They not only become familiar with a wide range of art media, tools, equipment, and techniques, but also express thoughts, values, and feelings.

Art criticism enables students to learn from works of art that have been created by artists from many cultures and time periods. It also provides a procedure that students can use to objectively study their own works of art.

The four foundational disciplines of art education are so flexible that they will carry art educators through the changes that are occurring in the post-modern era of art.

Integrating Fine Arts

Susan Cambigue-Tracey
Education Division, The Music Center of Los Angeles County

Albert Einstein said, "Imagination is more important than knowledge." Without exercising the imagination, knowledge is stored in the individual containers of the mind, but connections are not made. When students are taught to use the elements, skills, and content of the visual and performing arts, the possibilities for synthesizing and applying what they know are multiplied. Teachers need to ensure that imagination and creativity are always nourishing the roots of learning.

The importance of artistic activity for all students goes beyond the intrinsic value of each art form in itself, for real arts investigation requires the rigor of being able to focus, make decisions, develop discipline, promote originality, and undertake research, study, and practice. Helping students to experience new ways of thinking and seeing allows them to construct personal meaning from what they experience and build confidence and motivation.

Each art form is a discrete discipline with its own elements, vocabulary, and strategies. However, it is interesting to see connections between them where there are fundamental concepts shared across the arts and other subjects. For example, lines in art are the marks used to create images. Line in dance is the path of gestures and traveling movements, as well as body design. Line in music is a melody and also the lyrics of a song, while lines in theatre are the words that the actors speak.

A common core of knowledge is built through the arts. The principles of visual art, such as emphasis, variety, harmony, unity, and contrast are the underlying principles used to create anything—an architectural structure, a musical composition, a piece of literature, a dance, or a play.

> The importance of artistic activity for all students goes beyond the intrinsic value of each art form in itself, for real arts investigation requires the rigor of being able to focus, make decisions, develop discipline, promote originality, and undertake research, study, and practice.

It is easy to find ways to integrate one or more of the art forms and still make connections that are viable and authentic. For example, when viewing and discussing a work of art from a particular time period or culture, select music from that same time period or culture. Aztec art will have more relevance when Aztec-inspired music is played or students can view an Aztec dance and see the colors and design of the costumes. A style of music might also inspire art. Matisse created a Jazz series that begs for jazz music and dance. Students can then see and hear the structural and improvisational aspects of this style in three different art forms.

When viewing or painting family scenes in art, challenge students to think of family activities that can be portrayed in a tableau, or live, frozen picture. When viewing or creating sculpture, pair students up and have one person become the "clay" and the other the "sculptor" who shapes the clay with respect and cooperation. This can extend into dance by directing the sculpted person (clay) to develop a movement idea lasting eight counts that starts and ends with the sculpted pose or form. Two people in contrasting sculptural poses can have eight counts to slowly transform from one into the other.

Three-dimensional forms in art can inspire counterbalanced (push, pull, leaning) designs made by small groups. A story, such as "The Two Skyscrapers Who Wanted to Have a Child" by Carl Sandburg, could be retold using story theatre or be portrayed in tableaux or as dramatized scenes. Students could also research musical selections to accompany their work.

Students will be better able to express emotions in their visual artwork if they first work with their emotions through drama, music, and dance.

Students can begin by showing a variety of emotions in the face, hands, and feet, and then move toward portraying these emotions in postures such as sitting, standing, and walking. Everyday activities such as cooking or brushing teeth can be done with different emotional motivations. Students can also create short musical pieces depicting an emotion or mood or find music that expresses specific feelings or moods.

All four performing arts can become a powerful component of integrated learning. For example, a fifth-grade project focused on the Lewis and Clark Expedition. During a ten-week unit, students did research in books and on the Internet to collect historical, scientific, geographical, and cultural content. This information served as the basis for group projects in music, dance, theatre, visual arts, technology, and language.

Challenged by well-designed tasks, students discussed what they knew and selected different aspects to explore through dance, music, theatre, and visual art. They learned songs of the times, listened to traditional fiddle music, and learned a rhythmic chant that was used to measure the depth of rivers. In dances, they captured the sense of traveling through "boundless space"; portrayed animals the expedition encountered; created weather conditions such as storms; and showed the struggles faced in navigating rivers, waterfalls, and mountains. In theatre, students drew upon the historical characters, interpreted various scenarios, and dramatically read journal entries of Lewis and Clark. Visual art classes focused on observation drawings of plants and wild animals.

Students also created journals in which they recorded their feelings, observations, sketches, and discoveries. They were able to make connections between their own journeys and that of the Corps of Discovery. Finally, the students shared what they had learned about this epic journey in a multi-arts culmination.

The arts bring accessibility and vitality to learning, empowering students to construct meaning that has relevance for their lives. When children learn to draw, they learn to see. When children learn to act, they learn how it feels to be in different roles, cultures, and circumstances. When children learn to dance, they learn to feel comfortable within their bodies and to use movement expressively. When children learn to play an instrument, they learn perseverance and the rewards of expression through music. When children learn to sing, they release their voices and are empowered to harmonize. When children learn to write a play, they learn to observe life by thinking, reflecting, and writing. When creativity and imagination are nurtured, children learn how to use all of their resources to solve problems, to dream, and to build on the ideas of others.

Exhibiting Student Art

Jackie Ellett

"My picture is hanging in the hall!" exclaims an excited second grader. Yes, having one's work displayed is exciting! When you display a child's artwork you are communicating two things to that child; you value what he or she has created *and* you value the child.

Why Display Students' Art?

Students are intrigued by the work their peers produce and are eager to join in any discussion that arises from the shared experiences of the work. They often compare what they have created to the work made by their peers. A natural aesthetic experience occurs, and questions and comparisons arise. These are either verbalized or internalized depending on the circumstance of the viewing. "Why did Erin paint that flower large and the others small?" "I like the details of the seeds that Galvin added to his painting; I'll do more details next time." These are examples of questions, comments, or thoughts that may arise when viewing a display. Not only do displays allow students to appreciate their completed projects, but they also allow students to aspire to better art endeavors.

A class display allows students the opportunity to stand back and critique their work. A teacher-led critique is best. Students are able to evaluate their work, gain insight into things they may not have thought about, and they may learn a new solution to a problem they have encountered. Discussing their works as you would a fine art print validates the importance of what they have created. Art is so personal that a discussion can become quite insightful.

Preschool and early elementary-aged students are eager to take their works of art home to show their families what they have created. You should ask permission of any student to display their work. By asking permission you are showing respect for their work, and for that student as an individual.

Displays are also a good way to show administrators, families, and the community what the students are learning.

Where to Display Students' Art

Many art educators believe that the farther away from the classroom the display, the more selective the images need to be. In the classroom every student's art may be displayed. This area can be controlled by the teacher, student, or both. Students can be allowed to change their own work when they decide to.

Outside the classroom there is usually an assigned area for each class to display their work. Bulletin boards made of composition board are the most desirable of all surfaces for two-dimensional art. Artwork is easily attached using staples, and the walls are protected from any damage.

Setting up a school gallery of permanent or rotating student art is wonderful for promoting the art program within a school. This should be housed in a high-traffic area where families, administrators, and visitors can view the students' art. Having a gallery within the school with professionally matted and framed student art communicates that the students' works and the art program are valued. In an era where budget cuts are customary, promoting the work of our students is very important to the survival of the art program.

Displays in local businesses, civic centers, or art centers help educate the public as to what is taking place within area schools. These exhibits usually contain a mix of student art that has gone through a selection process. Depending on the guidelines and formality of the display, the works can be mounted, matted, or framed, with three-dimensional works displayed in sculpture cases or on sculpture stands.

How to Display Students' Art

Student art is displayed in a variety of ways. Some teachers take digital photos of their students in the process of creating a work of art and critiquing their work, and then take a photo of the finished art itself. These images can be posted on a school Web site with descriptions of the activity. Digital images are sometimes used as screen savers on the school's computer systems and highlighted on closed-circuit TV in the classrooms. The most common way, however, is the bulletin board. Bulletin boards have always been a part of teaching. They have evolved from simple displays to elaborate descriptions of the process and documentation of student learning. Teacher-focused bulletin boards have given way to student-focused displays that often include student reflections and interpretations. Including descriptions of the process and background information adds to better understanding of the learning that has taken place.

Two-dimensional work should be mounted on larger contrasting or neutral-toned paper. The top and sides are usually of equal width with the bottom larger, unless the work is square, in which case all four sides are equal in width. When matting art a two- to three-inch mat is standard, with the bottom being an inch wider than the top and sides. The mat acts as a resting place, so when arranging mounted or matted art, the images should not overlap.

A sheet of butcher paper or bulletin-board paper can be attached to the wall to define a display area and unify the artwork. Posterboard or construction paper cut wider on all sides than the largest paper used by a class can be attached to the wall as an area for mounting individual students' work. Glue a clothespin to the top of the mounted board or paper so students can easily change their artwork. The background papers are usually in neutral colors, although primary colors are often used in classrooms for younger children. These boards are individually identified by placing the child's name in large print on a label.

Three-dimensional works look best in sculpture cases or on sculpture stands. Not every school can afford these. Arranging sturdy boxes of varying heights and covering them with a complementary cloth allows sculptures to be equally viewed. If sculptures are of varying sizes, the largest should always be placed toward the back and the small works in front. Arranging works in odd numbers creates interest as well.

Mobiles and kites are best displayed from the ceiling. Make certain that all materials are well attached and that the items hung from the ceiling are secure so they do not fall or set off sensor alarms. As with all displays, it is important to know your school's policies about the types of adhesives allowed on the walls. Hot glue has a tendency to peel paint, low-temperature glue guns may not work on some surfaces, and double-sided tape can leave a residue. Humidity and the wall's surface both affect what will and will not work. The reusable tacky putty sticks to most surfaces and leaves few marks.

Displays do much to enhance and rejuvenate the spirit and allow students to communicate in a way that is neither mathematical nor verbal. The art that students make is very personal and deserves careful attention when being displayed.

> Students are able to evaluate their work, gain insight into things they may not have thought about, and they may learn a new solution to a problem they have encountered. Discussing their works as you would a fine art print validates the importance of what they have created.

Organizing the Art Room

A well-organized art room makes instruction, art production, and classroom management easier for students and teachers alike. Below are some tips for setting up different areas of the art room.

Production Area

Production tables should be arranged so that all students, including students in wheelchairs, can move freely between them. This also allows the teacher to move freely between the tables to help individual students. Tables may be arranged separately or in small groups to provide more surface area.

Listening Center

The purpose of this center is to have a place for discussions and demonstrations. Set up one area of the room where students can focus attention on you. Some teachers use benches or chairs arranged in a U shape. Another possibility is to use a large piece of carpet with sitting places designated by pieces of tape. There should be a wall with a bulletin board or a chalkboard on the fourth side of the U. The teacher can place a small desk or table in the center of the U so that the materials for the lesson can be explained.

Students can look at textbooks in the listening center instead of at the production tables; this keeps production materials from damaging the books. Discussions about the images and ideas on the book pages can be controlled in this group setting. Books may be left on the benches so students can go back and reference them during the lesson.

Although the students will be crowded, the arrangement of the listening center allows the teacher to control the group and to make eye contact with every child. The teacher can easily see if a student is not paying attention and can address the situation.

A listening center provides several benefits in the art classroom.

- It provides a place for students to sit when they enter the room. If students go directly to the tables where materials are set up for the production activity, their attention will be on the art materials and not on the teacher.

- It provides a place to hold discussions with the students about art history, art criticism, and aesthetic perception. Fine art prints and other posters can be placed on the wall where students can see them clearly. This is the place where the lesson begins.

- It provides a place where the teacher can model new techniques. The arrangement of the center allows each student to see the demonstration.

- It provides a place where students who finish early can go to draw or use art game materials while other students finish their work at the tables.

Display Area

Every art room should include an area for displaying both two-dimensional and three-dimensional student art. Covering the wall with corkboard or a similar surface allows the display to be set up and changed easily. Three-dimensional art should be displayed in cabinets whenever possible. Try to display every student's art, and include master works in the display. This gives students a sense of achievement and helps build self-confidence.

Storage

The art room should provide two kinds of storage. Books, student portfolios, paper, and similar items can be kept on low shelves that are accessible to students. Keeping these shelves organized and labeled will help students return materials to the correct place during cleanup. In classrooms with younger students, include pictures on the labels as well as words. Other supplies and equipment can be kept in lockable storage cabinets or a separate room.

One way to organize student materials is to color code portfolios, journals, and so on. For example, all of the first-grade classes could have books and portfolios that are blue, second-grade classes could have yellow, and so on. The teacher can mark attendance and grading pages with colors to match. If there are several first-grade classes, the teacher might give every class a different color. This color coding system also helps substitute teachers locate necessary information.

Museum Resources

Carol Henry

Art museums are excellent resources for teaching art. Of course, a field trip to an art museum is a wonderful opportunity for your students to see original art in a space designed especially for that purpose. The art is displayed free from ordinary distractions. Everything about the space, from the placement of the work to the lighting to the text on the walls, is designed to help the viewer make connections with the work of art. Studies have shown that students remember such experiences in great detail, in part because the experience is so different from the typical, everyday school experience. Arranging field trips in current financial times can seem like a daunting experience, but the end result is well worth the effort. Even if you are unable to schedule a field trip due to financial, educational, or geographic restraints, art museums can still be exciting resources to help you enrich your instruction and address specific visual arts standards.

Today, good art education practice centers on the belief that it is important to provide students with the opportunity to view and respond to works of art as well as to be involved in the production of art. This belief is evidenced in the National Standards for Arts Education (NAEA, 1994), which address what "every young American should know and be able to do in the Arts" (p. 18). According to these standards, students should be able to "communicate proficiently" in the visual arts, "develop and present basic analyses of works of visual art, have informed acquaintance with exemplary works of art from a variety of cultures and historical periods, and be able to relate art knowledge within and across the arts disciplines" (p. 14), all aspects of current museum education programming.

As art teachers, we can first teach our students about museums. What are their purposes? Who are they for? Why do people visit them? In such discussions, students can learn that museums serve to collect, protect, display, and help interpret works of art for the public. Students can also learn that what a museum collects reflects the values of that museum and of our culture as a whole. They can also think about art in other contexts, such as public art within our communities. Through this type of instruction, we can help students see that museums can be inviting spaces, open to all, for providing opportunities for continuous learning experiences throughout their lives.

> Students can learn that museums serve to collect, protect, display, and help interpret works of art for the public. Students can also learn that what a museum collects reflects the values of that museum and of our culture as a whole.

The Internet makes it possible for you and your students to "visit" many museums, right in your classroom. One elementary teacher I know regularly takes her students on a "virtual tour" of the Louvre in Paris (www.louvre.fr). Although these children live in a small town in northern Georgia, they have gained an understanding of the famous museum and its collection. In fact, one student who actually traveled to the Louvre with his parents was able to tell them where the entrance was based on his experiences in his third-grade art class. Even more importantly, he was able to connect his experience with what he had learned in that class. Another excellent site that allows you to develop a variety of "virtual" field trips is the National Gallery of Art in Washington, D.C. (http://nga.gov). The Metropolitan Museum of Art in New York also has options for educational tours (www.metmuseum.org). These are but a few of the museum Web sites being used by teachers across the country; an Internet search will lead to many more.

Museum Web sites are also a valuable source for educational resources designed especially for classroom use. The resources frequently take the form of "teacher packets" and are typically developed to accompany important exhibitions.

These packets include reproductions of important works in the exhibition, sometimes as slides but more frequently as color overhead transparencies or full-color posters for classroom use. Historical background information and suggestions for student learning experiences are also included. The Chicago Art Institute, the Seattle Art Museum, the High Museum of Art in Atlanta, the Philadelphia Museum of Art, and the National Gallery are but a few of the museums known for the quality of these materials. The resources are generally affordable and can be purchased as part of your yearly ordering of supplies or as part of your media center's annual book order. In some cases, museums offer teacher workshops, and these materials are provided as part of that workshop. Check with museums in your area to find out if workshops are being offered that relate to aspects of your curriculum. Museums with strong educational missions are aware of the importance of working with teachers to develop these materials and, as a result, there may be opportunities for you to voice your opinion through service on a teacher advisory panel, developing lessons, or field-testing materials.

If you decide to schedule a field trip, develop a strong, educational rationale for the experience. You do have to convince administrators that there is educational value beyond increasing appreciation of art. The fact that works of art allow us access to other cultures, provide opportunities to explore ideas important throughout history, and allow us important insight into ourselves and others is not necessarily universally understood. It is your job to communicate these ideas and the education standards such an experience would address. Once you have received the approval you need, certain things will help the trip be even more successful. Always visit the exhibit first in order to develop instruction that is designed to prepare your students for the art they will encounter. Learning is most likely to occur when it connects to previous experience. You can request a docent tour, and, in such cases, provide any information you can about your students that will help the docents make connections to your students. Each museum has different policies for such visits; it may be possible for you to take a group through yourself. In any case, develop an assignment that allows your students to reflect on the experience once you have returned to the classroom.

Introducing students to art museums is an important part of teaching art. Museums are often conceived of as formal, austere environments by those who do not visit them. As a teacher, you can make your students aware of the relevance of museums and their potential for personal engagement throughout students' lives. At the same time, you will be enriching your curriculum through access to a vast array of educational possibilities.

Arts Advocacy

Mini Course

Take this short quiz to identify your strengths and weaknesses in arts advocacy. Choose the best answer for each question.

Research

1. Research on the effects of arts education has shown which of the following?

   a. Arts education causes students to score higher on standardized tests.
   b. There is a correlation between arts education and higher standardized test scores.
   c. Arts education has no impact on standardized test scores.
   d. None of the above

2. Which of the following is supported by research?

   a. Visual art has no impact on reading.
   b. Incorporating visual arts into other curriculum areas has a negligible impact on student motivation.
   c. Skills used in visual arts training can also be applied to scientific images.
   d. Dramatizing text does not aid reading comprehension.

3. Arts education strengthens which of the following skills?

   a. Risk taking   b. Problem solving
   c. Creative thinking   d. All of the above

4. Visual arts training encourages _____.

   a. circular reasoning
   b. evidential reasoning
   c. problematic reasoning
   d. none of the above

Parent and Community Involvement

5. Arts advocacy efforts can involve _____.

   a. students   b. parents
   c. other teachers d. all of the above

6. Advocacy efforts should include information about _____.

   a. the skills students practice when learning about art
   b. why art is better than other subjects
   c. ways to integrate art with other subjects
   d. none of the above

7. Student artwork can be displayed in _____.

   a. libraries   b. local businesses
   c. school display areas d. all of the above

Grant Writing

8. Grants are available from _____.

   a. the federal government
   b. state governments
   c. private companies
   d. all of the above

9. Grant readers want to know _____.

   a. which art supplies you will purchase with the grant money
   b. where else you have applied for grants
   c. how your proposal will support education
   d. grants you have received in the past

10. The first step in writing a grant application is _____.

    a. determining what students would learn and how it could be achieved
    b. obtaining an official application form.
    c. enlisting the help of a professional grant-writer
    d. checking with your school board

. . . .

Scoring:
If you answered all the questions correctly, you have a good understanding of arts advocacy.

If you missed all the questions in one section, you might want to read the applicable article in order to achieve a better understanding.

If you missed more than seven questions, you could benefit from more information on arts advocacy. Consider reading all of the articles in the Arts Advocacy section to get a better understanding.

Answers: 1. b, 2. c, 3. d, 4. b, 5. d, 6. a, 7. d, 8. d, 9. c, 10. a

38   Professional Development Guide

Arts Education Research Overview

Art educators have known for a long time that art education fosters creativity, critical thinking, decision-making skills, self esteem, and other valuable skills. However, several studies and research compendiums have emerged recently that document these benefits as well as other positive results of art education.

Test Scores

- Data from a National Educational Longitudinal Study (NELS) showed a relationship between arts involvement and high test scores. This held true for students across all socio-economic levels.

- Research suggests that when arts are integrated in schools, students tend to perform better on standardized reading and math tests. This seems to be especially true for low socio-economic status students at the elementary school level.

- Students involved in the arts showed higher reading proficiency, higher standardized test scores, and a lower dropout rate than non-arts-involved students. These results hold true across grade levels and across socio-economic status levels.

- One study showed that students on average gained eight percentile points on a standardized language arts test after one year of learning in an arts-integrated classroom and gained sixteen percentile points after two years.

Connections to Other Subject Areas

- Research has shown that incorporating the arts into core curriculum areas in a way that actively involves students in the learning process has a positive impact on student motivation and achievement.

- Young children who dramatize text improve their reading comprehension.

- One case study showed that reluctant readers were better able to engage in reading when the creating and analysis of visual art was incorporated into their story discussions.

- Research has shown that the perception and thinking skills learned during visual art training can also be applied to scientific images.

Cognitive Skills

- Artistically talented students engage in more self-regulatory behavior in classes with arts integration than in classes without it. These behaviors include paying attention, problem solving, asking questions, taking risks, and so on.

- Students involved in visual arts training have shown less circular reasoning and more evidential reasoning when evaluating both fine art images and scientific images.

- Students in after-school arts-based programs gain practice in working with adults to plan, develop, and execute ideas that they rarely receive in any other context. These are valuable workplace skills.

- High-arts students outscore low-arts students on measures of creative thinking, elaboration, and resistance to closure.

Learning Environment and Self-Concept

- One large study demonstrated that students involved with the arts were "less likely to drop out of school, watched fewer hours of television, were less likely to report boredom in school, had a more positive self-concept, and were more involved in community service."

- Students involved in the arts are more likely than non-arts-involved students to perceive themselves as academically competent.

- When students study art forms from minority cultures, this instruction seems to diminish stereotypes about that culture.

Resources

ArtsEdge: Articles and Reports (http://artsedge.kennedy-center.org/connect/rpt.cfm)

Champions of Change: The Impact of the Arts on Learning. Edward B. Fiske, ed. Washington, D.C.: Arts Education Partnership.

Critical Links: Learning in the Arts and Student Academic and Social Development. Washington, D.C.: Arts Education Partnership. 2002.

Schools, Communities, and the Arts: A Research Compendium. Tempe, AZ: Morrison Institute for Pubic Policy. 1995.

Arts Advocacy with Parents and the Community

Art teachers know that their job often involves not only teaching art, but also advocating arts instruction to parents, community officials, and the general public. Following are some suggestions for making parents and community members aware of the value of arts education.

Start with Students

Encouraging students to share their experiences in art class with their families can be one of the best ways to show parents the benefits of arts education.

- Ask students to tell their parents what they learned in art class. How did they use the elements and principles of art in their project? What techniques did they learn? What decisions did they make as they worked on the project?

- When you send home permission slips and so on, include arts advocacy information on the form. Keep the statements short and to the point.

- Send home an art newsletter with students. This can range from a short description of what students are learning in class to a more elaborate newsletter that includes pictures of student artwork. Remember to describe not only the creative thinking and production skills that students are learning, but also the critical thinking, decision-making, and teamwork skills that students are developing as they progress through the year.

Involve Parents

Once parents realize the value of art education, they can become advocates for your art program.

- When parents have positive comments about their child's art experience, encourage them to share their comments with other parents, the principal, or the superintendent.

- Make parents aware of school board meetings where art is on the agenda. Encourage parents to attend these meetings and share their views on the importance of art education.

- Organize a parent art group. This can be an independent group or can be part of your local parent-teacher association. Parent volunteers can help set up and promote student art shows, coordinate and publish the art newsletter, and raise awareness of art events in the community.

Be Visible in the Community

- Whenever possible, display student artwork in public places. Libraries, civic buildings, and local businesses are often willing to display student art. Have students write a few sentences about what they learned and display their statements with the artwork.

- When possible, coordinate student artwork with community events.

- Submit notices of upcoming art events to your local newspaper or radio station, and include your name as the contact person. (Media contact information may be available from your local chamber of commerce.) Send invitations for these events to school and community leaders, and send a follow-up note to those who attend.

- Advocate art education at every opportunity. Local civic associations, service groups, and so on often invite speakers to their meetings. Share your students' accomplishments and describe what they are learning in art class.

Following these steps can help raise awareness of the importance of art education with parents, principals, school board members, community leaders, and other decision-makers.

Grant Writing

Mary Lazzari, EdS
Elementary Art Teacher, Clarke County School District, Athens, Georgia

The greatest successes in education are the result of collaboration. Art educators are uniquely qualified to make connections between people, ideas, and materials that inspire new discoveries. Strong art programs build upon resources within the community, and this includes financial assistance. There are numerous public and private organizations that are eager to support schools. A quick search of the Internet yields over three million sites for educational grants and another one million sites for art education grants. Unfortunately, many art teachers feel intimidated, scared, or overwhelmed by the grant writing process. They are unclear about where to find grants or believe that the grant writing process is difficult. Applying for a grant is no more complex than organizing your curriculum or writing lesson plans.

It is best to approach grant writing the way you plan for a new art activity. First organize your thoughts: 1) What will the students learn? 2) How will this be achieved? 3) What materials are required? Ask colleagues and associates to critique your idea before you even begin to write the application. Also enlist the expertise of a professional grant writer. Many school districts have a grant writer on staff to apply for and manage large state and federal funding. Make sure your project is simple enough for a non-arts person to understand. When writing the proposal you should always start with the most important point. Make sure your objectives are clear, easily measured, and include state or national art standards.

It is also a good idea to write your budgetary plan early and then make sure your proposal supports every item in it. Some common expenditures include materials and equipment, school-wide events, field trips, artists-in-residence, and special projects. When writing grants to purchase equipment, be sure to discuss the number of students that will make use of these resources. Remember, as an art teacher your grant has the potential to impact several hundred students. Other grantors are interested in how your proposal will support education. Use grant money to support school or state initiatives within your art curriculum. If improving reading goals or math achievement scores is a school-wide goal, write your grant to purchase fine art literature or math and art integrated resources.

> Art educators are uniquely qualified to make connections between people, ideas, and materials that inspire new discoveries.

To be successful, art teachers should look for grants that best suit their goals and writing expertise. Novice grant writers may be unsure how to find and contact these granting agencies. First look for grants in your own backyard. Applying for private grants is easier than applying for federal or state grants. Check for grants in your school district or local community. Many corporations, philanthropic groups, and non-profit agencies offer grants to schools. Learn about the organization sponsoring the grant. Know the grantor's priorities and tailor your proposal to fit their objectives. Grant readers are interested in how their money will be used to benefit students and how it will support the community.

Key elements of grant writing are:

- **Title:** *Make it descriptive and creative to catch the grant reader's imagination.*

- **Introduction:** *Why are you writing this grant? What is the purpose? Identify the individuals or agency involved. Describe the needs of your school or local community.*

- **Need or problem:** *Who is your target group? What evidence has been collected to justify the need for this project? Describe your capability to solve this problem.*

- **Goals:** *What do you wish to achieve? Describe the outcome of the project in terms of the problem.*

- **Objectives:** *What steps will you take to reach this goal? Make sure they are measurable, realistic, and manageable.*

- **Procedures:** *How do you plan to reach your goals? Describe specific activities and tasks. Relate all activities to your objectives.*
- **Evaluation:** *How will you show you have reached your goal? Describe the process and methods for measuring the project's effectiveness.*
- **Budget:** *Clearly list and explain all totals. Consider the resources you will need to meet this goal. Include shipping costs or travel expenses, if applicable.*

Many grants provide you with a format and application sheet to be completed. It is important not to deviate from a grantor's required format. If your grant application does not give a specific layout, do your best to make it look appealing and reader friendly. Proposals should be typed using a 12-point font and double-spacing. Ask a friend or associate not directly involved with the project to proofread your proposal. Have him or her check for grammatical errors, logical inconsistencies, and unjustified budget items. You should know the deadline requirements and send your application using certified mail. This will provide you with a receipt showing when it was mailed and notification that your grant proposal was received.

A common thread weaving itself through education is collaboration between schools and community partners. A school's effectiveness is directly tied to these collaborative efforts. The financial support that can be derived from community partnerships is important to the strength and diversity of the art curriculum. Writing grants can help art teachers expand their programs and establish relationships with enthusiastic community partners. The more grants you attempt, the greater your chances for success. Writing grants can be a worthwhile endeavor with long-lasting results that benefit students, teachers, and the community.

Web Resources

Americans for the Arts
www.artsusa.org/default.asp

Provides a wealth of information for teachers, administrators, community leaders, and parents. Site contents include news, educational resources, community development, and funding information.

Art Education Page for K–12
http://falcon.jmu.edu/~ramseyil/arteducation.htm

Provides links to sites about general art education, art history, museums, artists, art of various geographic and cultural regions, and techniques. Also includes links to sites with activities and lesson plans.

Art History Resources on the Web
http://witcombe.sbc.edu/ARTHLinks.html

Contains comprehensive links to information about art history around the world.

Art Teacher on the Net
www.artmuseums.com/

Contains information on art projects (including projects for adults), art history, and parent ideas. Also includes a teacher exchange board with questions and answers.

Arts and Learning Resources for State Leaders
www.nasaa-arts.org/nasaanews/al_research.htm

Contains links to sites about education, arts and learning, and educational approaches, among others. Compiled by the National Assembly of State Arts Agencies.

ArtLex
www.artlex.com/

A dictionary of art terms, including illustrations and cross references.

ArtsEdge
http://artsedge.kennedy-center.org/

Sponsored by the Kennedy Center for the Performing Arts, this site provides teacher resources (including lessons and standards), advocacy information, and content about individual artists and art topics.

ArtsEdNet
www.getty.edu/artsednet/

Sponsored by the Getty Museum; contains lesson plans, gallery and exhibition information, and ArtsEdNet Talk, an online group of art teachers and students.

Artsnet
www.artsnet.org/

Includes a directory of art sites on the Web as well as a list of online arts management resources.

Center for Educator Development in Fine Arts
http://finearts.esc20.net/default.html

Texas-based site provides instructional strategies and other information useful for teachers in all states.

Coming Up Taller
www.cominguptaller.org/inside.html

Sponsored by the President's Committee on the Arts and the Humanities; provides links to art programs for at-risk students, resources, and arts enrichment programs.

The Educator's Reference Desk
www.eduref.org/cgi-bin/res.cgi/Subjects/Arts

Formerly AskERIC. Contains information on advocacy and assessment as well as lesson plans and activities.

The Louvre
www.louvre.fr/

Home page of the Louvre in Paris. (Text is in French, but a link to the English version is available after the opening screen.)

The Metropolitan Museum of Art
www.metmuseum.org/explore/index.asp

Online educational resources at The Metropolitan Museum of Art.

National Art Education Association
www.naea-reston.org/

The home page of the National Art Education Association; contains news, advocacy information, publications, and information on special programs.

National Endowment for the Arts
http://arts.endow.gov/

Includes grant information as well as other information on the visual and performing arts.

National Museum of Women in the Arts
www.nmwa.org/

Home page of the National Museum of Women in the Arts in Washington, D.C.

National Standards for Visual Arts Education
www.getty.edu/artsednet/resources/Scope/Standards/

Part of the Getty ArtsEdNet. Contains the national content and achievement standards, as well as a scope and sequence.

National Conference of State Legislatures: Arts & Culture
www.ncsl.org/programs/arts/arts.htm

Provides information about arts education and funding in the states.

Smithsonian Institution
www.si.edu/

Home page of the Smithsonian Institution. Contains links to the Smithsonian museums, including the Cooper-Hewitt Museum, the American Indian Museum, and the Freer Gallery of Asian art.

Notes

Notes

Notes

Notes